Airline
Nostalgia

Airline
Nostalgia
CLASSIC AIRCRAFT IN COLOUR

Adrian M. Balch

Photograph Index

Copyright © 1999 Adrian Balch

First published in the UK in 1999
by Airlife Publishing Ltd

ISBN 1 882663-42-X

Typeset by Rowland Phototypesetting Ltd, Bury St Edmunds, Suffolk.
Printed in Hong Kong.

Distributed in the U.S. and Canada by Plymouth Press, 101 Panton Road, Vergennes, VT 05491. To order additional copies or for a free catalog, call 1-800-350-1007.

INTRODUCTION

You've all heard the joke, 'Nostalgia isn't what it used to be'. Humans are strange creatures, and we love to look back and reminisce in the past. When times seem bad, we like to recall 'the good old days' and aviation enthusiasts are no exception. The dictionary defines 'nostalgia' as 'sentimental yearning for a period of the past' and 'regretful or wistful memory of an earlier time'. It doesn't matter what age you are, you will always have a period in aviation to look back on with fond memories. Recalling days of propliners at airports on long hot summer days is a favourite memory and it is hoped that something in this book will evoke that feeling of airline nostalgia. This is the companion to *Vintage Glory*, also available from Airlife Publishing. If you enjoyed that book, then here is another helping of the same material to complement it. Likewise, if you enjoy what you see here, then look for *Vintage Glory*, or write to Airlife for a copy.

Once again, this book would have been impossible to produce from my own cameras alone and I have to thank some very good friends around the world. Particular thanks go to Werner Gysin-Aegerter, Stephen Wolf, Bernard B. Deatrick, Tom Cole of the Boeing Commercial Airplane Co., Brian Stainer of Aviation Photo News and Tony Eastwood of The Aviation Hobby Shop (TAHS). Those photographs credited to the latter are available as original 6″x 4″ colour prints, together with many more .
For a full list, write to

The Aviation Hobby Shop,
4, Horton Parade,
Horton Road,
West Drayton,
Middlesex,
England UB7 8EA

I have spent many hours on the roof terraces of London's Heathrow Airport with my father in the early 1960s, soaking up the sights, sounds and smells of a variety of classic airliners of the same time. I feel very privileged to have subsequently flown in some of the types featured in this book, including the Douglas DC-3, Bristol Britannia, de Havilland Comet, Boeing 707, Vickers Viscount and Ilyushin Il-14, among others.

Seeing, recording, photographing and experiencing all these classic airliners was a wonderful experience, which cannot be repeated in many cases. Remembering them by looking through this book, can only be summed up in one word – 'nostalgia'.
Now turn the pages and share those memories.

Adrian Balch
January 1999

Below: Luton-based Autair International changed its name to Court Line on 1 January 1970. The airline used a fleet of seven BAC One-Eleven 400/500s on a wide range of international charters to holiday resorts throughout the Mediterranean region. With a new name came a new image, the aircraft painted in combinations of turquoise, pink, orange and lilac. On 15 August 1974, the airline declared itself bankrupt and ceased trading. BAC One-Eleven 518FG G-AXMH (c/n 202) is seen here outside the Bournemouth-Hurn factory on 25 January 1970, prior to delivery. It was one of four painted in the two-tone orange scheme and was named *Halcyon Sun*. It was re-registered G-BDAS in February 1975 and sold to Dan-Air, which in turn ceased trading in 1992. In October 1994, this aircraft was re-registered G-OBWB with British World Airlines, with whom it is current.

(*Stephen Wolf*)

Opposite above: Here is a typical scene at Gatwick Airport in June 1976, with Dan-Air's BAC One-Elevens, G-ATPJ and 'TPL, sandwiching British Airways' Vickers V.806 Viscount G-APEX. In the distance can be seen two BAC One-Elevens of Laker Airways. The nearest Dan-Air One-Eleven is Series 301AG, G-ATPJ (c/n 033), which was originally delivered to British Eagle in June 1966. Dan-Air bought it in March 1970. When the company ceased operation, it went to Chilean operator Ladeco Airlines in November 1990 and was withdrawn from use at Santiago in November 1994.

(*Author's collection*)

Opposite below: Convair 880 N814TW (c/n 22-00-19) is seen here on finals to Los Angeles in October 1963, two years after its delivery to Trans World Airlines. It was withdrawn from use in January 1974 and sold to American Jet Industries in June 1978. Following corporate and cargo service, it was finally withdrawn from use in June 1983 and has been stored to this day at Mojave, California.

(*Werner Gysin-Aegerter*)

Below: Transvalair's Canadair CL-44, HB-IEO (c/n 32), is depicted with just inches to go before touch-down at Basel on 14 April 1979. One of two Canadair CL-44s operated by this airline, it was originally registered as N229SW of Seaboard World Airlines, then leased to Transglobe Airways as G-AWOV, before being sold to Tradewinds Airways in June 1970. Transvalair acquired it in December 1977, selling it in October 1979. It was last reported withdrawn from use in June 1983 at Tripoli, Libya, after service with United African Airlines.

(*Werner Gysin-Aegerter*)

Opposite above: Passengers boarding Martin 4-0-4, N40430 (c/n 14136), at Richmond, Virginia, in October 1963. Piedmont Airlines bought this aircraft from Trans World Airlines in December 1961 and named it *Chesapeake Pacemaker*. It was sold in December 1968 and was last heard of impounded at Sebring Airport, Florida, in February 1983 and is presumed broken up.

(*Werner Gysin-Aegerter*)

Opposite below: Loftleidir (Icelandic Airlines) operated five DC-6Bs throughout Europe and across the Atlantic. TF-LLC (c/n 44121), named *Thorfinnur Karlsefni*, was bought from Pan American World Airways in March 1961 and is depicted here at Idlewild Airport, New York in September 1963. It was leased to Transavia in December 1968 and was last operated by the Peruvian Air Force. The aircraft was withdrawn from use and stored in August 1970.

(*Werner Gysin-Aegerter*)

Below: PH-VIB (c/n 173) was one of nine Vickers V.803 Viscounts operated by KLM during the late 1950s and early 1960s. Named *Louis Blériot*, this particular machine was delivered on 26 July 1957 and was sold to Aer Lingus as EI-AOJ in December 1966, along with the rest of the fleet. It is seen here taxying at Köln-Bonn in March 1966. It was withdrawn from use with Aer Lingus on 1 November 1970, and was broken up at Dublin in January 1973.

(Werner Gysin-Aegerter)

Bottom: Aer Lingus was an early customer for the BAC One-Eleven and EI-ANH (c/n 052) was the last of four Series 208ALs to enter service in 1965. Named *St Ronan*, it is seen here in its original livery at Manchester in June 1967. It was sold to Guinness Peat Aviation in July 1991, becoming 5N-HTB when leased to Hold Trade Air. All four One-Elevens gave faithful and reliable service to Aer Lingus for twenty-five years.

(Author's collection)

Above: Powered by two Shvetsov radial piston engines, the Ilyushin Il-14 was built in large numbers in the Soviet Union. All of the Eastern Bloc countries operated a handful of these, including Poland. SP-LNA of the Polish airline, LOT, is seen here taxying at Zürich-Kloten in September 1963.

(*Werner Gysin-Aegerter*)

Below: This photograph of the cockpit of an Ilyushin Il-14, shows it to have more room and better visibility than the DC-3 or Convair 440. This is one of the few still airworthy in Russia in 1997.

(*Adrian Balch*)

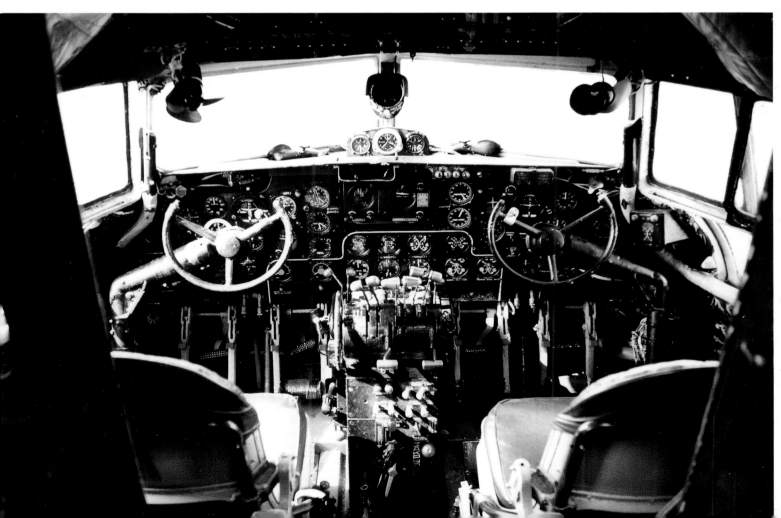

Below: The fleet of twelve SPANTAX Convair 990As was a familiar sight throughout Europe during the 1960s and 1970s. EC-BTE (c/n 30-10-21) is seen here taxying in at its home base of Palma, Majorca, on 22 March 1976. It was originally delivered to American Airlines as N5609 in March 1962 and bought from Modern Air Transport by SPANTAX in March 1970. It was withdrawn from use and stored at Palma in October 1981.
(*Adrian Balch*)

Opposite above: This ultra low-level flying shot shows Air UK's BAC One-Eleven 408AK G-CBIA (c/n 166) leaving from Bournemouth-Hurn on 17 December 1979 in its original Air UK livery. For safety reasons, this livery had to be modified, as it was thought hazardous to fly an all-blue aircraft in a blue sky, so this scheme was short-lived. British Island Airways merged with Air UK in January 1980 when G-CBIA had just been repainted at Hurn. It was originally delivered to Autair International as G-AWXJ and in October 1989 was sold to Okada Air as 5N-AYW.
(*Stephen Wolf*)

Opposite below: SE-CCZ (c/n 43830), named *Uppsala*, was one of a pair of Douglas DC-6Bs purchased from SABENA in early 1963 by Transair of Sweden. It is seen here at Barcelona on 11 July 1963 with KLM's DC-7C PH-DSC behind. 'CZ was sold in December 1965 and was last operated as OO-VGB of Delta Air Transport, when it was damaged beyond repair at Southend, Essex, on 4 October 1974. It was broken up three months later.
(*Author's collection*)

Below: The distinctive shape of an Air France Breguet 763 Deux Ponts was photographed on finals to Marseille in March 1967. F-BASN was actually c/n 1 and the first of twelve used by Air France on passenger and freight flights throughout Europe. This actual machine was converted to a Universal freighter in 1965 and withdrawn from use in June 1971.

(Werner Gysin-Aegerter)

Opposite above: The two Bristol Centaurus piston engines cough and splutter as another load of British holidaymakers arrive at Palma, Majorca, in Dan-Air Airspeed Ambassador G-ALZN (c/n 5212) in September 1964. This was one of ten originally operated by British European Airways and acquired by Dan-Air in April 1962. It was withdrawn from use in May 1968 and broken up at Lasham, Hampshire.

(Werner Gysin-Aegerter)

Opposite below: Very similar to the Avro 748, the Japanese NAMC YS-11A was common in the Far East. However, the only European airline to operate the type was Olympic Airways, who took delivery of ten in 1971 for domestic services, including SX-BBP (c/n 2153), named *Isle of Andros*. It was one of six sold to the Greek Air Force in November 1980 and is currently withdrawn from use at Elefsis, being used as a source of spares to keep the last two airworthy.

(Andy Heape)

Opposite above: G-ASEN was one of five Douglas C-54 Skymasters operated by Manston-based Invicta Airways, joining the airline in February 1966 from ACE Freighters. It was converted to cargo use in June 1969 and was sold to Africair in February 1971. The following year it was broken up at Bulawayo, Rhodesia (now Zimbabwe). It is seen here taxying at Zürich in November 1969. (*Author's collection*)

Opposite below: Ghana Airways operated two Bristol Britannias during the early 1960s, including this Series 319, 9G-AAH (c/n 13207), seen here at Heathrow in 1963. It was originally delivered to BOAC as G-AOVA and was sold to Ghana Airways in November 1960 who operated it for just three years before it was passed on to British United Airways, British Eagle and Caledonian Airways. It was finally withdrawn from use at Coventry and reduced to spares in October 1971. (*Author's collection*)

Above: A classic in its element – Lockheed L1649A Starliner LX-LGZ (c/n 1041) was one of three operated by Luxair. It is seen here on finals to Palma, Majorca, in September 1964. It was originally delivered to Lufthansa in January 1958. Luxair then leased it from the South African airline, Trek Airways between April 1964 until May 1967. It was eventually withdrawn from use at Johannesburg, South Africa, in September 1969 and broken up the following year.

(*Werner Gysin-Aegerter*)

Above: Channel Airways placed an order for five de Havilland Trident 1Es in October 1967, but this was later reduced to just two. G-AVYE (c/n 2139) was delivered to the airline in June 1968 and it is seen here at Southend just two months later. It was sold to BEA in January 1972, who in turn sold it to Northeast Airlines in November 1973. This airline merged with British Airways on 1 April 1976 and 'VYE was finally retired to the Science Museum collection at Wroughton on 24 April 1981. Replaced in the collection by a Trident 3, 'YVE was broken up in June 1989. (*Bob Griggs*)

Opposite above: United Arab Airlines operated a fleet of nine de Havilland Comet 4Cs, of which SU-ALC (c/n 6439) was the first. Originally called Misrair, the airline took delivery of this aircraft on 10 June 1960 and changed its name to United Arab Airlines six months later. This aircraft saw ten years' service before crashing at Ben Gashir, near Tripoli, Libya, on 2 January 1971. It is seen here at an unknown location in 1965. (*Author's collection*)

Opposite below: Full power on – British European Airways' (BEA) Comet 4B G-APMA (c/n 6421) begins its take-off run at Heathrow in September 1968. Named *Sir Edmund Halley*, it was delivered to BEA in December 1959, serving all its life with the airline until being scrapped at Heathrow in 1969. Note the light grey lower fuselage, which was painted over the polished natural metal during the mid-1960s. (*Bob Griggs*)

Below: Eagle Airways was formed on 14 April 1948, initially named Eagle Aviation. The airline survived for twenty years, its titles changing from Eagle Airways, through Cunard Eagle Airways to British Eagle International Airlines, finally ceasing operations in November 1968. Douglas DC-6A G-APSA (c/n 45497) is seen here at Heathrow in the Eagle Airways livery circa 1959. It was bought from Maritime Central Airways in September 1958 and sold to Saudi Arabian Airlines in February 1964. It was acquired by Yemen Airways in 1971, then purchased by Air Atlantique in February 1987. It currently flies as G-APSA from Coventry in Atlantic Cargo colours on freight duties throughout Europe. (See page 95) *(Brian Stainer/APN)*

Opposite above: Here is another Douglas DC-6B, one of eight operated by Norwegian operator, Braathens SAFE. LN-SUB (c/n 45496) is seen on a misty day at Gatwick in October 1969. Braathens bought this machine from Cathay Pacific Airways in November 1962 and sold it in May 1971. It is still flying in Canada as a fire-bomber with Conair Aviation. *(Bob Griggs)*

Opposite Below: An unidentified Braniff International Douglas DC-7C stands at Dallas, awaiting its next load of passengers in 1965. Braniff operated six DC-7Cs during the late 1950s and early 1960s from its base at Dallas to points throughout the US. The DC-7 did not survive in Braniff service to see the airline's radical change in livery. *(Author's collection)*

Opposite above: Douglas DC-7C EC-BSQ (c/n 45159) of SPANTAX claws its way into the air at Basel, Switzerland, in August 1971, bound for a Spanish holiday destination. It was originally OO-SFC of SABENA and was sold to SPANTAX in January 1970. It was withdrawn from use at Las Palmas, Canary Islands, in 1979. (*Werner Gysin-Aegerter*)

Opposite below: EC-BJK (c/n 44874) was one of three Douglas DC-7Cs operated by Spanish charter airline Trans Europa, which was formed in 1965 and ceased operations in February 1982. This particular DC-7C is seen about to depart Basel, Switzerland, in September 1971. It was originally N732PA of Pan American World Airways. It was acquired by Trans Europa in May 1967 and served the airline until being broken up at Madrid in November 1974. (*Werner Gysin-Aegerter*)

Above: Monarch Airlines' Bristol Britannia 312 G-AOVI (c/n 12926) arrives at Basel, Switzerland, in August 1970 with another holiday charter flight from Luton. Originally delivered to BOAC in February 1958, Monarch bought this aircraft from Caledonian Airways ten years later in February 1968. After just four years' service with the airline, it was broken up at Luton in January 1972. (*Werner Gysin-Aegerter*)

Above: The Bristol Britannia was built under licence in Canada as the Canadair CL-44, re-engined with Rolls-Royce Tyne turboprops and equipped with a swing-tail cargo door. However, the American company, Conroy, modified one of these aircraft still further to carry outsize loads. Known as the Conroy CL-44-0 Guppy, N447T (c/n 16) was originally delivered as a standard CL-44 to Flying Tiger Line Inc. After conversion by Conroy in November 1969, it was delivered to Transmeridian Air Cargo on lease. Named *Skymonster*, it operated from Stansted. It was sold to Heavylift Cargo Airlines in October 1982, registered EI-BND and then served Buffalo Airways in December 1993. N447T is seen here at Basel, Switzerland, in November 1970.

(*Werner Gysin-Aegerter*)

Above: Swiss Air Lines Douglas DC-3, HB-IRN, is illuminated by late afternoon sun at Basel in April 1964. It was one of the last three DC-3s operated by Swissair and was once KN683 of the RAF. On 1 July 1972 it was retired and transferred to the Transport Museum at Lucerne, where it is beautifully preserved to this day. (*Werner Gysin-Aegerter*)

Opposite above: A typical Swiss winter scene – Balair's Douglas DC-6B HB-IBZ (c/n 44089) awaits snow clearance at Basel in February 1968. Originally delivered to Swissair in November 1953, it was transferred to Balair in December 1961. It was then sold to the Zaire Air Force in December 1971, withdrawn from use in 1980 and broken up the following year.
(*Werner Gysin-Aegerter*)

Opposite below: With the famous mountainous scenery of Geneva in the background, Balair's Fokker F27 Friendship 100, registered HB-AAU (c/n 10200), completes another internal flight in March 1967. Originally D-BAKE of LTU, it was sold to Balair in March 1965, then in April 1972 became PH-KFC of the Dutch airline, NLM. It was last reported with Aviation Assistance, withdrawn from use and stored at Roskilde, Denmark, in January 1993.
(*Werner Gysin-Aegerter*)

Below: Texas International's Convair 600 N94235 (c/n 68) taxies out at Dallas in September 1972. This was one of twenty-five piston-engined Convair 240s re-engined with Rolls-Royce Dart turboprops. The aircraft in the background is one of the airline's piston-engined Convair 440s. This particular machine was originally delivered to American Airlines in April 1948 and sold to Trans Texas Airways in September 1964. The aircraft was converted in 1967 and the airline was renamed Texas International on 31 October 1968. The aircraft was last reported as withdrawn from use and stored at Tucson, Arizona, but may well be broken up by now.
(*Werner Gysin-Aegerter*)

Below: OD-AFI (c/n 30-10-35) was one of six Convair 990A Coronados operated by Middle East Airlines (MEA). It was originally N5603 of American Airlines and was sold to MEA in July 1969. In March 1971, it was bought by SPANTAX as EC-BXI and was finally withdrawn from use at Palma, Majorca, in June 1981.
(*Author's collection*)

Opposite above: Ecuatoriana's Lockheed Electra HC-AYL (c/n 1031) taxies out at Miami in September 1972, bound for Quito. Ecuatoriana was the first of the smaller airlines to acquire used Electras, with the first arriving in 1967. At one point the airline was using six Electras in regular service, but services declined in 1973 and the remaining aircraft were transferred to the military airline, TAME. This particular machine was originally N6107A of American Airlines, delivered in February 1959. After service with National Airlines and several leasing companies, it was acquired by Ecuatoriana in June 1972 but returned to the leasing company in March the following year. It was withdrawn from use at Miami in June 1976 and broken up two years later.

(*Werner Gysin-Aegerter*)

Opposite below: Compagnie Air Transport operated a cross-Channel car ferry service in association with British Air Ferries from June 1961. Three Bristol 170 Superfreighter Mk 32s were used, including F-BLHH, which is seen here at Basel, Switzerland, in April 1968. This particular aircraft, c/n 13212, was previously G-ANWH of Silver City Airways and was subsequently leased to Cie Air Transport and British United Air Ferries. Its last flight was on 11 June 1969, when it was damaged beyond repair at le Touquet, France.

(*via Werner Gysin-Aegerter*)

Below: The unique French 'double-decker' was the Breguet 763 Deux Ponts, of which twelve were built for Air France. F-BASV (c/n 9) was delivered on 24 March 1954 and was converted to a Universal freighter in 1965. Once a regular visitor to Heathrow, it was withdrawn from use in January 1969 and scrapped at Toulouse in August. It is seen here taxiing at Nizza in March 1967.
(Werner Gysin-Aegerter)

Opposite above: G-APWB (c/n 150) was one of five Handley Page Heralds operated by Luton-based Autair International. It served for three years from November 1966 to November 1969, following service with BEA. In November 1970, just before the airline changed its name to Court Line it was sold to La Urraca of Colombia, with whom it crashed at Villavicencio on 2 November 1973. It is seen here at Basel, Switzerland, in March 1968.
(via Werner Gysin-Aegerter)

Opposite below: Lufthansa made subtle changes to its livery during the operation of its eleven Vickers V.814D Viscounts. D-ANAM (c/n 368) is seen here taxiing at Zürich-Kloten in 1965 with a straight plain blue cheatline, without the yellow borders and blue nose of the original livery. It was delivered in April 1959, serving all its life with Lufthansa, and was withdrawn from use at Hamburg in July 1970. It was preserved in October 1976.
(via Werner Gysin-Aegerter)

Below: The Tupolev Tu-104 was a fairly rare sight outside the Soviet Union, but the smaller Tu-124 was even rarer. It had a fuselage 16 ft shorter than the former and a wingspan that was 9 ft shorter. Named 'Cookpot' by NATO, the Tu-124 first flew in June 1960. About one hundred were built for Aeroflot and small numbers were also used by CSA, Interflug, Iraqi Airways and the Indian Air Force. Aeroflot's SSSR-45092 is seen here taxiing at Vienna in September 1966.

(*Werner Gysin-Aegerter*)

Opposite above: The Ilyushin Il-14 was Russia's answer to the Convair 240. Based on the inferior Il-12, the Il-14 first flew on 20 September 1950. From 1958, Avia built two hundred Il-14s, of which twenty-four were delivered to the national airline, CSA (Ceskoslovenske Aerolinie). The airline was formed in 1923 and OK-MCP displayed the 45th anniversary markings when it was photographed at Paris in June 1969.

(*Author's collection*)

Opposite below: Austrian Airlines was an early customer for the Avro 748, purchasing just two in early 1966. OE-LHT (c/n 66) named *Anton Bruckner*, was sold to Philippine Airlines in September 1970. However, it was destroyed after a fire on take-off, 5 km south of Manila Airport on 3 February 1975. It is seen here in its original Austrian colours, taxiing at Vienna in September 1966.

(*Werner Gysin-Aegerter*)

Opposite above: Olympic Airways was the only overseas customer for the Comet 4B variant. This model featured the long nose of the Comet 4C combined with the short wing of the Mk 4, but was devoid of external tip tanks. Olympic Comet 4B operations commenced on 18 May 1960, its fleet of four comprising two Greek-registered machines and two British-registered, leased from BEA. G-ARJL (c/n 6455) was one of the latter and was leased to Olympic between February 1964 to February 1970. It was finally purchased by Dan-Air for spares and broken up at Lasham in September 1974. It is depicted here on finals to Frankfurt in March 1966.

(*Werner Gysin-Aegerter*)

Opposite below: This scene is the perfect Christmas card setting for any nostalgic aviation enthusiast. Swissair's Convair 440 Metropolitan HB-IML (c/n 365) taxies in at Geneva in January 1965. This was one of eleven Convair 440s operated by Swissair between September 1956 to October 1968. Incredibly, in 1997 it was still in service with North East Bolivian Airways, who purchased it in 1979.

(*Werner Gysin-Aegerter*)

Above: Morton Air Services was formed in May 1945 and operated Douglas DC-3s and de Havilland Herons throughout the UK and across the Channel during the 1960s. Based initially at Croydon, then later at Gatwick, the airline survived until 1 November 1968, when its aircraft were either transferred to British United Airways or sold. De Havilland Heron G-AOXL (c/n 14015) is seen here at Gatwick in September 1965. It was purchased in May 1957 and retained until the airline merged with British United Island Airways. It was last reported as withdrawn from use and stored in Norway. Note the DC-7C in the background, belonging to Dutch charter airline Martin's Air Charter, later becoming Martinair.

(*Werner Gysin-Aegerter*)

Below: G-ASIV (c/n 45310) was one of seven Douglas DC-7Cs operated by Caledonian Airways from Gatwick during the early 1960s. Named *County of Midlothian*, it was leased from SABENA and is seen here taxying out at Gatwick in September 1965. This aircraft, originally registered as OO-SFJ, ended its days being broken up at Basel, Switzerland, in 1980, after being seized by the airport authorities in 1971.

(*Werner Gysin-Aegerter*)

Opposite above: Here is a sight to make any propliner enthusiast's pulse race – a 'Super Connie' on approach. This is actually one of Iberia's L1049G Super Constellations, EC-AQN (c/n 4645), on finals to Palma, Majorca, in September 1964. Iberia operated seven of these during the early 1960s. This was originally PH-LKK of KLM (see *Vintage Glory*, page 48) and was sold to Iberia in August 1962. It ended its days while being operated on Biafra relief flights, crashing on approach to Port Harcourt, Biafra, in January 1968.

(*Werner Gysin-Aegerter*)

Opposite below: PH-DSL (c/n 45180) was one of sixteen Douglas DC-7Cs operated by KLM during the 1950s and early 1960s. Named *Baltic Sea*, it was delivered to KLM in April 1957 and was then sold to Martin's Air Charter (see *Vintage Glory*, page 67) in November 1964. It was withdrawn from use at Stansted, Essex, and broken up in 1981. It is seen here on finals to Palma, Majorca, in September 1964.

(*Werner Gysin-Aegerter*)

Opposite above: This classic 'Connie' shot features Lufthansa's L-1049G, D-ALEM (c/n 4603) arriving at Palma, Majorca, in September 1964 with another load of German holidaymakers. It served all its life with Lufthansa from its delivery on 19 April 1955 until its withdrawal from use at Hamburg. It was broken up in March 1967.

(*Werner Gysin-Aegerter*)

Opposite below: SABENA operated nine Boeing 707-329s during the 1960s and early 1970s including OO-SJF (c/n 18374), which is seen in this April 1967 ramp view at Heathrow Airport. Notice the period BEA vehicles assisting the turn-round. This particular aircraft was delivered to SABENA in April 1962 and leased to several airlines before becoming 4X-BYL of the Israeli Air Force in 1977, with whom it is current.

(*Brian Stainer/APN*)

Below: Air India's Boeing 707-437s began operating the Bombay–London service on 19 April 1960. These were later supplemented by the Boeing 707-337 variant with extended range, including VT-DSI (c/n 18873), seen here on finals to Kai Tak Airport, Hong Kong, on 25 March 1980. In more than twenty years of Air India's Boeing 707 operations, there were only subtle changes to its livery. VT-DSI was actually delivered to March 1965 and was sold back to Boeing in September 1989 for spares use. It was broken up at Davis Monthan, Arizona.

(*Adrian Balch*)

Below: South African Airways (SAA) commenced a Johannesburg to London service with a Boeing 707 on 14 September 1960. Initially, a trio of aircraft was used, but later the fleet was increased to eight. Boeing 707-344B ZS-SAE (c/n 19133), named *Windhoek*, is seen here overflying Cape Town in 1970 with Table Mountain in the background. This particular aircraft was delivered to SAA in January 1967 as ZS-EKV and was re-registered the following year. It was sold to Air Mauritius in April 1983, then leased to several airlines. It was sold back to Boeing for spares in October 1990 and was subsequently broken up at Davis Monthan, Arizona.
(*South African Airways*)

Opposite above: This photograph features an unidentified Boeing 707-436, thought to be G-ARRC (c/n 18413), wearing BOAC-CUNARD titles at Heathrow in May 1966. The Cunard Steamship company formed a partnership with the British Overseas Airways Corporation on 6 June 1962, taking a thirty per cent interest to operate Atlantic services. Cunard Eagle's Boeing 707s passed to BOAC on 28 September 1962 and BOAC-CUNARD was formed, together with eight of BOAC's Boeing 707s. The partnership was broken up on 15 October 1966.
(*Author's collection*)

Opposite below: The first Boeing 727s in Europe were those delivered to Lufthansa, who commenced operations with the type on 16 April 1964 on the Hamburg–London–Düsseldorf route. The initial order for Lufthansa comprised twelve Boeing 727-30 variants, including D-ABIF (c/n 18363), seen here at Rome in October 1964. This aircraft is currently registered as EP-PLN with the Iranian Government.
(*Author's collection*)

Below: British European Airways (Channel Islands Division) operated Vickers Viscounts up until the formation of British Airways on 31 July 1973. G-AOHV (c/n 170) was a Series V.802, which was delivered new to BEA in July 1957 and continued with British Airways until March 1980. Its final operator was British World Airlines, who retired it from service in 1993. G-AOHV is seen here at Glasgow in September 1972, awaiting another load of passengers.

(Author's collection)

Opposite above: Austrian Airlines initially ordered six Vickers Viscounts in February 1960, but later increased the number to twelve. V.837 Viscount OE-IAM (c/n 442) was initially registered OE-LAM when delivered in August 1960, but was re-registered when leased to Austrian Air Transport. Named *Ludwig V. Beethoven*, it was finally sold in October 1971. It was destroyed after a mid-air explosion on 21 January 1972, after take-off from Bogotá, Colombia. OE-IAM is seen here at Brussels on 11 April 1970.

(Author's collection)

Opposite below: Maitland Drewery Aviation was founded early in 1959 by J. R. Maitland and W. E. Drewery who joined the company the following year. Based at Biggin Hill, the company soon expanded and operated from Gatwick. Two Viscounts were acquired in June 1960, including V.708 G-ARBY (c/n 010), which is depicted here at Biggin Hill in 1961. The aircraft were leased to BKS Air Transport during the summer of 1961, following which the Viscounts were leased to Silver City Airways, who were absorbed by British United Airways. The aircraft were sold to BUA in December 1961 and Maitland Drewery ceased operations.

(Author's collection)

Below: Viscounts in BOAC colours were rare. V.701 G-AMOG (c/n 7) was one of two Viscounts leased from Cambrian Airways in the early seventies to operate a daily Prestwick–Edinburgh link to back up BOAC's transatlantic services. Named *Scottish Prince*, G-AMOG was originally delivered to BEA in March 1953. Cambrian bought it ten years later, then leased it to BOAC from October 1972 until the formation of British Airways on 1 April 1974. On 27 April 1976, this aircraft was donated to the Cosford Aerospace Museum, where it can be seen today in a representation of its original BEA colours. This photograph was taken at Edinburgh-Turnhouse in 1972.

(Author's collection)

Opposite above: Vickers Viking G-AHPM (c/n 152) was originally delivered to BEA in March 1947 and was sold to Eagle Aviation in July 1953. Operating from Blackbushe, then Heathrow, it served in Eagle Airways' colours (the airline being renamed Cunard Eagle Airways in January 1961) until it crashed in Norway on 9 August 1961. All thirty-nine occupants were killed. G-AHPM is depicted here at Heathrow in 1960.

(Author's collection)

Opposite below: Vickers V.745D Viscount VP-YTE (c/n 243) was one of ten operated by Air Rhodesia. Previously owned by Middle East Airlines and registered as OD-ADD, it joined Air Rhodesia in July 1970. The airline changed its name to Air Zimbabwe in September 1981 and in January 1990 this aircraft was sold to Trans Service Airlift, with whom it still serves. It is seen here in Air Rhodesia service at Kariba, Rhodesia (now Zimbabwe), in February 1975.

(Dave Lawrence)

Below: XU-JTA was one of two Sud-Aviation SE-210 Caravelle IIIs that Royal Air Cambodge bought from Air France in January 1969. These titles only lasted for one year, following which the 'Royal' was dropped. It is seen here at Hong Kong's Kai Tak Airport in the company of a Lufthansa Boeing 707 and a Japan Air Lines DC-8 on 18 March 1969. This aircraft was destroyed in a communist attack on Phnom-Penh, Cambodia, on 22 January 1971.
(*Bernard B. Deatrick*)

Opposite above: BOAC's Vickers Super VC 10 G-ASGB (c/n 852) sweeps in to land past BEA's Engineering Base on 8 August 1974 – a classic Heathrow scene. This photograph was soon not able to be repeated, as British Airways was formed on 1 April 1974 when BEA and BOAC merged, changing the markings on this aircraft and building. Both were overdue to be altered. Delivered in April 1965, G-ASGB was one of twenty-five Super VC 10s operated by BOAC and subsequently British Airways. It was sold in April 1981, being allocated the RAF serial ZD231. However, after a long storage at Abingdon, it was broken up for spares in March 1987.
(*Adrian Balch*)

Opposite below: Utilising its former Air Canada red cheatline and tail colour scheme, Invicta International's Vickers Vanguard G-AXDY (c/n 727) still looks pristine, sitting at Luton on 21 February 1975. It was originally delivered as CF-TKD in December 1960 to Trans-Canada Airlines, which changed its name to Air Canada on 1 June 1964. In July 1969 it was sold to Air Holdings who leased it out to various cargo airlines before it was sold to Manston-based Invicta International Airlines in March 1973. In November 1975 it was sold to Europe Aero Service as F-BXOH, but never flew in their colours. It was broken up at Perpignan, France, shortly after.
(*Adrian Balch*)

Below: This Danish-registered Caravelle III, OY-KRF (c/n 170), is depicted being turned round by period vehicles at London Heathrow Airport in April 1967. Named *Torkil Viking*, this aircraft was a regular visitor in Scandinavian Airlines System's livery. It ended its days with China Airlines, being withdrawn from use at Taipei, Taiwan, in October 1979. Note the excellent spectators' viewing facilities from the Queen's Building at Heathrow in the background (sadly little more than a memory now).

(*Author's collection*)

Opposite above: After using three earlier Caravelle IIIs for a number of years, Finnair bought ten of the upgraded Caravelle 10B3s in 1966, including OH-LSG (c/n 169). Named *Jyvaskyla*, OH-LSG is seen here at Amsterdam-Schiphol on 2 July 1973. The year this photograph was taken is reflected by the roof legend, as Finnair was celebrating its 50th anniversary. The Finnair Caravelles were long-serving and reliable, eventually being sold in June 1984. This was one of the last Caravelles, flying in 1993 with Air City as HB-ICJ.

(*W. F. Wilson*)

Opposite below: An airline no longer seen in Britain, Libyan Arab Airlines operated just three Caravelles from July 1965 until they were withdrawn from use at Tripoli, Libya, in 1976. Wearing the airline's smart gold livery, 5A-DAB (c/n 162) is a Caravelle VIR and is seen here basking in the sun at Rome, Italy, in October 1970.

(*Author's collection*)

Above: Pacific Northern Airlines operated three Boeing 720s on its Seattle to Anchorage route, with the first one being delivered in 1962. All three were transferred to Western Airlines during a merger in 1967. Boeing 720-062 N720W (c/n 18377) is seen here prior to delivery on 18 April 1962. After service with Western Airlines, it was passed on to Alaska Airlines and Pan American World Airways. It was finally withdrawn from use at Berlin-Tempelhof in July 1976 and broken up two years later.

(*Boeing*)

Above: Somewhat rarer than the similar Convair 440, this Martin 4-0-4, registered N468M (c/n 14139), was one of four operated by Ozark Airlines when it was photographed at Waterloo, Iowa, in December 1966. The fleet was disposed of the following year and this example continued to serve with several operators, until being broken up at Fort Lauderdale, Florida, in October 1978.

(*Author's collection*)

Below: The Curtiss C-46 Commando was always a rarity in England, N9891Z (c/n 33242) was leased from Capitol Airways by Lufthansa between March 1964–November 1969, and it is seen here on a freight charter, visiting Heathrow in 1966. More than thirty years later, this aircraft still flies in Canada as C-FAVO with Buffalo Airways.
(*TAHS*)

Above: D-ABOH was the first of eight Boeing 720-030 variants to join Lufthansa. Seen here on a pre-delivery test flight over Washington in early 1961, its career with the airline was short-lived, as it was sold to Pan American World Airways in March 1964. In July 1973 it was sold to Avianca Colombia, and it was finally withdrawn from use and broken up at St Petersburg, Florida, in 1981.

(*Boeing*)

Below: A classic Heathrow scene in the early days of British Airways' formation was photographed on 31 March 1974, featuring Boeing 707-336C G-ASZF (c/n 18924) still surrounded by BOAC vehicles awaiting a repaint. On 19 December 1965, this aircraft was delivered new to BOAC, which officially became British Airways the day after this photograph was taken. It was sold to a Nigerian cargo airline in May 1983, and promptly written off at Accra, Ghana, on 25 September the same year.
(*Adrian Balch*)

Opposite above: Trans-Canada Airlines (TCA) was the first North American customer for the Vickers Viscount. The company started with a Montreal–Toronto–Lakehead–Winnipeg route on 1 April 1955 and eventually had more than fifty in service all over Canada. TCA changed its name to Air Canada in 1964 and all the Viscounts adopted the new livery until the last one was retired in April 1974. V.757 Viscount CF-THC (c/n 220) is seen awaiting its next load of passengers at Sea Island, Vancouver, on 5 April 1964.
(*Bernard B. Deatrick*)

Opposite below: The unmistakeable classic lines of the Vickers VC 10 can be seen as G-ARVG of Gulf Air sweeps in to land on London Heathrow's Runway 28L on 8 August 1974. This aircraft was delivered to BOAC on 12 June 1964 and went on to serve with British Airways after the merger with BEA on 1 April 1974. It was initially leased to Gulf Air in June 1974, the airline purchasing the aircraft the following year and amending the registration to A40-VG. This aircraft still flies today as a tanker with the Royal Air Force as ZA141 with 101 Squadron at Brize Norton.
(*Adrian Balch*)

Above: With a puff of smoke and a squeal from the tyres, Air Canada Cargo's Douglas DC-8F-54 C-FTJL (c/n 45640) touches down at London Heathrow on 14 April 1979. Air Canada DC-8s served London Heathrow for twenty-five years from June 1960, formerly as Trans-Canada Air Lines and then from 1 June 1964 as Air Canada. This particular machine was one of six DC-8F 'Jet Traders' and served with the airline from April 1963 to December 1984. It still flies in Venezuela with Zuliana Air.

(*Adrian Balch*)

Left: G-AOII was one of ten Douglas DC-7Cs operated by BOAC and was delivered on 29 January 1957. It was converted to a DC-7CF in December 1960 as shown here and was acquired by SAS in 1965, becoming OY-KNE. It was last reported at Miami, serving Conner Air Lines and is now withdrawn from use.
(*TAHS*)

Left: Handley Page Herald CF-EPI (c/n 166) was one of four operated by Eastern Provincial Airways in Canada and was delivered in January 1963. It is seen here at Charlottetown, Prince Edward Island. It was sold to British Air Ferries in January 1975, becoming G-BCWE. In April 1988 it was bought by Aerovias SA of Guatemala, becoming TG-ASA, and was last reported withdrawn from use.
(*TAHS*)

Below: Starways was based at Liverpool and bought two Viscounts from Air France, operating them from 1961 until the company ceased operations on 31 December 1963. Vickers V.708C Viscount G-ARIR (c/n 036) was originally delivered to Air France as F-BGNS. It was finally operated by MMM Aero Service in Zaire, before being broken up at Ostende, Belgium, in December 1988. It is seen here at Heathrow in 1963.

(*The Aviation Hobby Shop files*)

Bottom: G-ALAK (c/n 2548) was one of the five Lockheed L.794A Constellations operated by Gatwick-based ACE (Aviation Charter Enterprises) Freighters during 1965–66. Most of the revenue came from Ministry of Defence charters from Lyneham and Abingdon to the Middle and Far East. G-ALAK is seen here visiting Heathrow in 1965. The following year, ACE Freighters ceased trading and was the last operator of the Constellation on the UK register. G-ALAK ended up being scrapped at Miami in 1971, last registered as OB-R-899 of the Peruvian airline, COPISA.

(*The Aviation Hobby Shop files*)

Above: High over the snow-covered New Zealand mountains is Fokker F27 Mk 500 Friendship ZK-NFA (c/n 10551), which was one of fifteen of the type used on domestic flights by New Zealand National Airways Corporation (NAC). The airline started operations in 1947 and in March 1977 this Friendship was delivered new to the airline thirty years later. This photograph was taken seven months later on 2 October 1977. NAC changed its name to Air New Zealand on 1 April 1978, so this colour scheme was short-lived. In February 1992, this aircraft was sold to the Indonesian airline, Merpati Nusantara Airlines.

(*John Mounce*)

Right: Here we see the same aircraft photographed in 1978 after refurbishment and overhaul by Fokker-VFW. It is wearing the new Air New Zealand livery, together with the Dutch registration, PH-EXA, for test flights over Holland.

(*via John Mounce*)

Below: The ideal combination of snow and sunshine produced this fine shot of Eastern Airlines' Lockheed Electra N5528 (c/n 1045) at La Guardia, New York, in February 1977. Eastern was the third carrier to order Electras, after American and National. They ended up operating forty of the type and N5528 gave nearly twenty years service to Eastern from its delivery in April 1959 until being sold in December 1977, along with the rest of the fleet. Alas, it was damaged beyond repair in a forced landing 120 km from Kinshasa, Zaire, on 5 February 1986, registered 9Q-CWT.
(*Author's collection*)

Opposite above: This is not a Boeing 737, but the second of only twelve Dassault Mercures, all of which were only operated by Air Inter. F-WTMD (c/n 02) first flew on 7 September 1972 and is seen here taxying at Le Bourget during the Paris Air Show in June 1973. With no further sales, the type was an expensive loss for Dassault. The whole fleet had a safe and uneventful career, all being withdrawn from use in 1995.

(*Dave Cross*)

Opposite below: In 1965 Braniff International revolutionised the traditional airline colour scheme of white roof and coloured cheatline, by painting the whole fuselage of its aircraft in one of seven colours, with white flying surfaces. Here – blue Lockheed Electra, N9704C (c/n 1086), is seen at Kansas awaiting its next load of passengers in October 1967. This aircraft was delivered new to Braniff in August 1959 and served the airline faithfully for ten years, until being sold to Peruvian operator, LANSA, in August 1970. In LANSA's hands it crashed in Peru on Christmas Eve 1971.

(*Harry Sievers*)

Above: Although Eastern bought DC-8s for its long-haul routes, it also ordered Boeing 720s for shorter routes. Ten of these aircraft were leased from the Prudential Insurance Company for ten years, but were actually purchased by Eastern in 1966. All the Boeing 720s were traded-in to Boeing in 1969/70 when Boeing 727s were delivered. N8702E (c/n 18156) was the second Boeing 720-025 delivered, and is depicted here in its original 'Golden Falcon' livery on a pre-delivery test flight over Washington in August 1961.

(*Boeing*)

Above: The Curtiss C-46A Commando was a rare visitor to Britain and N10427 (c/n30532) of Seaboard World Airlines is seen here in 1966 on one of those rare visits to Heathrow. Originally delivered to the USAAF, Seaboard & Western Airlines acquired it in August 1956, the airline later changing its name to Seaboard World Airlines in April 1961. The aircraft was withdrawn from use at Frankfurt in 1970 and operated by a couple of private owners before crashing in Colombia in February 1973.

(*The Aviation Hobby Shop files*)

Above: Named *Princess Everetta Maria II*, Boeing 377 Stratocruiser YV-C-ERH (c/n 15931) of the Venezuelan Airline, RANSA, was photographed at Miami in the early 1960s. It was originally N1031V of Pan American World Airways, delivered to the airline in May 1949. It was sold to RANSA in April 1961 and was withdrawn from use at Miami in July 1969.

(*The Aviation Hobby Shop files*)

Above: This Convair 240, registered N94278 (c/n 163), was delivered to American Airlines in October 1950. It was then sold to Trans Texas Airways in December 1964 and in September 1966 was converted to Convair 600 standard with Rolls-Royce Dart turboprops. Its current status is unknown.
(*TAHS*)

Below: Until this photograph emerged, it was not thought that any of Eastern Airlines' Douglas DC-7s survived in service to adopt the two-tone blue 'hockey-stick' colour scheme. Possibly, N829D (c/n 45338) was the only one and it is seen here arriving at Washington National in 1965. It was sold the following year and broken up in 1970.

(*TAHS*)

Below: The swing-tail Canadair CL-44s of Seaboard World Airlines were familiar visitors to Heathrow throughout the 1960s, resplendent in their black and tan trim. Seaboard operated seven CL-44s, of which N123SW (c/n 30) was delivered on 5 April 1962. It became G-AWGT with Transglobe Airways in April 1968 and was leased to Tradewinds in November 1968, then to Cyprus Airways in June 1979. It crashed and was written off at Akrotiri, Cyprus, on 4 November 1980.

(*TAHS*)

Above: Boeing 720-023 N7527A (c/n 18013) is depicted in 1960 during a test flight prior to its delivery to American Airlines. It was handed over on 30 July 1960 and named *Flagship Mississippi*. At its peak, this carrier operated the largest number of Boeing 707s/720s in the world. This particular machine was withdrawn from use in July 1971, but continued in service three years later as G-BCBB with Invicta Airlines. After a series of leases, it was finally sold to the Israeli charter company, Maof Airlines, in October 1981, becoming 4X-BMB. It was bought by Israeli Aircraft Industries for spares in December 1985 and broken up at Tel Aviv in June 1986.

(Boeing)

Left: De Havilland Comet 2E G-AMXK (c/n 06033) was delivered to BOAC in August 1957, but only served for four months before being transferred to the Ministry of Supply. It was delivered to the Royal Aircraft Establishment at Farnborough in November 1966, becoming XV144. It was withdrawn from use in 1974 and broken up the following year.
(*TAHS*)

Left: This Vickers V.804 Viscount, registered SP-LVC (c/n 248), was one of three operated by LOT. It was originally G-AOXU of Transair and British United Airways before being sold to LOT in December 1962. It served the airline for four years before being sold to NZNAC in January 1967. It was only withdrawn from use on 15 October 1996 at Southend, after serving with British World Airlines as G-CSZB.
(*TAHS*)

Right: The colour scheme on Gulf Aviation's Douglas DC-3 G-AGKE reveals its association with BOAC. It saw service with Aden Airways as VR-AAB before joining Gulf Aviation on 13 April 1961. It was last reported as derelict in October 1978 at Bahrain.

(*TAHS*)

Right: Airspeed As57 Ambassador G-AMAC (c/n 5225) was acquired by BKS Air Transport from BEA in June 1960 and was operated on scheduled and charter flights in the United Kingdom and Europe until July 1968. The initials BKS came from the airline's founders, Messrs J. W. Barnby, T. D. Keegan and C. J. Stevens, together with Capt. J. P. Falconer. They founded the airline on 12 October 1951, which was subsequently renamed Northeast Airlines on 1 November 1970, then absorbed into British Airways on 31 March 1976.

(*TAHS*)

Above: On 1 February 1964, Eastern became the first airline to introduce the Boeing 727 on the Miami – Washington – Philadelphia route. The initial order was for twenty-five of the type, of which N8102N (c/n 18253) was the second Boeing 727-25, delivered on 15 November 1963. It is seen on a pre-delivery test flight over Washington in its original 'Jet Falcon' livery of blue, gold and red. It was sold in August 1982 to the government of Liberia and was finally broken up at Laurinburg, North Carolina, in February 1989.

(*Boeing*)

Right: Braniff International revolutionised airline colour schemes in the mid-1960s by painting its aircraft fuselages in one of seven colours, with all other surfaces remaining white. BAC One-Eleven Series 203AE N1545 (c/n 019) was painted turquoise and delivered in this scheme on 12 May 1965. It was last reported as still flying in Texas as an executive jet. *(TAHS)*

Right: Vickers 639 Viking 1 G-AGRV (c/n 114) was originaly delivered to British European Airways in August 1946. It was acquired by Hunting-Clan in May 1951, sold to Tradair of Southend in May 1960, and broken up in June 1960. *(TAHS)*

Above: The BAC One-Eleven was another British airline success in view of the fierce competition from the American DC-9. PI-C1121 is a One-Eleven 402 (c/n 091) and is seen here in its original Philippine Air Lines (PAL) livery at Manila on 6 January 1967. PAL initially took delivery of two One-Elevens in 1966, but they were so successful that many more were ordered. This particular aircraft is still flying, after being sold to the Ministry of Defence in May 1974, becoming XX919 with the Royal Aircraft Establishment at Bedford and the Defence Research Agency at Boscombe Down, with whom it is current.

(*Bernard B. Deatrick*)

Above: The distinctive and colourful livery of Ethiopian Airlines is one of the few that has hardly changed over the years. It is therefore difficult to date this superb shot of Boeing 720-060B ET-AAG (c/n 18454), which was actually taken just prior to the aircraft's delivery on 2 November 1962. This was one of a pair of the airline's first jet airliners, which served the airline's scheduled services to Madrid and Nairobi. It served faithfully until being destroyed by fire following a landing accident at Beirut, Lebanon, on 9 January 1968.

(*Boeing*)

Above: A typical scene at Luton, photographed during the hard winter of January 1963. Vickers Viking 1A G-AGRW (c/n 115) is in cargo configuration with Autair International who acquired the aircraft from Overseas Aviation in January 1962. Autair International was the last operator, withdrawing it from use in August 1964. Originally delivered to BEA in August 1946, this aircraft is currently preserved at Vienna, Austria.
(*TAHS*)

Above: Frontier Airlines was formed in June 1950 by the merger of three smaller airlines. Its first Boeing 727 went into service in late September 1967, just prior to the company absorbing Central Airlines the following month. Frontier traded in its original Boeing 727-100s for Boeing 737s, but took delivery of four Boeing 727-200s in February and March 1968. Boeing 727-291 N7276F (c/n 19991) is depicted just prior to its delivery on 8 February 1968. It was operated for four years before being sold to Braniff International in March 1972. Frontier Airlines ceased operations in 1985.

(*Boeing*)

Above: Twenty-five years before the current controversial British Airways colour schemes were thought of, this is the original colour scheme in which their first 'Jumbos' were delivered. BOAC (British Overseas Airways Corporation) took delivery of its fourth Boeing 747-136, registered G-AWND (c/n 19764), on 28 February 1971 in this smart dark blue and gold livery. It is seen here arriving at Jan Smuts Airport, Johannesburg, on 19 January 1973 on a scheduled flight from London. On 1 April 1974 BOAC merged with BEA to form British Airways. Unfortunately, 'November Delta' got caught up in the Gulf War and was impounded by Iraqi forces at Kuwait City on 2 August 1990 and was destroyed during the fighting on 27 February 1991. (*Andy Heape*)

Following spread: Several companies attempted to update the piston-engined Convair 440 with turboprop engines, the definitive version being the Convair 640, which was equipped with two Rolls-Royce Dart turboprops. PH-MAL (c/n 332) of Dutch charter airline, Martinair, began its life in June 1956 as Convair 440 HB-IMC of Swissair. Ten years later, Martinair bought it and converted it to the Convair 640 variant seen here at an unknown wintery location in February 1968. (*Author's collection*)

Below: Vickers Viking G-AJFT of Air Safaris was photographed at Gatwick in 1961. It was bought from Airwork Services in May 1960 and sold to Eros Airlines in March 1962. It ended its days with the Gatwick Airport Fire Service in September 1963.
(*The Aviation Hobby Shop files*)

Opposite above: A very rare visitor to Birmingham-Elmdon was photographed in December 1965. CUBANA's sole Antonov An-12, CU-T827, was on a freight charter.
(*The Aviation Hobby Shop files*)

Opposite below: Douglas DC-4 Skymaster N54373 (c/n 10273), named *Wake Island Airtrader*, was operated by Seaboard & Western Airlines from February 1953 until May 1959, when it was sold to Interocean Airways as LX-BNG. In August 1962, Aviation Traders converted it to an ATL-98 Carvair and it became G-ASDC with British United Air Ferries. It is currently one of the last airworthy Carvairs, flying in Alaska as N103.
(*The Aviation Hobby Shop files*)

Opposite above: This Misrair pair, SU-AOL (front) and 'AOM (rear), were rare Antonov An-24 visitors to London Heathrow. They were photographed in October 1967, operating an Egyptian charter service.

(*Brian Stainer/APN*)

Opposite below: This Viscount was delivered to British European in March 1958. In March 1984, it was operated by British Air Ferries who leased it to Guernsey Airlines until June 1987. Named *Viscount Guernsey*, G-AOYG was one of two Viscounts to wear this smart green variation of the BAF livery. The aircraft was finally withdrawn from use at Southend in December 1992 and was broken up in January 1994.

(*Courtesy British World Airlines*)

Above: Northeast Airlines operated twelve Boeing 727s, six of the shorter 100 Series and six of the longer 200 series. The first was delivered in October 1965 and N1632 (c/n 18858) was the second Boeing 727-95, seen here on a pre-delivery test flight in December 1965. The livery featured was short-lived, as Northeast changed to its yellow/white 'Yellowbird' scheme the following year. Northeast Airlines was taken over by Delta Air Lines on 1 August 1972.

(*Boeing*)

Opposite above: This exotic vintage scene was photographed at Téhran, Iran, in September 1962 and features an aircraft of Trans Mediterranean Airways. Originally delivered to BOAC in September 1945 as G-AGNP, this Avro York ended its days shortly after this photograph was taken. It crashed seven miles south-east of Karaj, Iran on 15 March 1963.

(*Norman Ling*)

Opposite below: This Northeast Airlines line-up features Douglas DC-9-15 N8953U (c/n 45797), flanked by a Douglas DC-6 in the foreground and a Fairchild F27 behind. The setting is Logan International Airport, Boston, in February 1967. The DC-9, delivered new the previous year, was then leased to Delta Air Lines and is now a corporate executive transport.

(*Author's collection*)

Above: A Convair airliner still flying in the 1990s was this Allison turboprop-powered Convair 580, C-FNRC (c/n 473), operated by the Canadian National Research Council on radar research trials. It has a radar nose and wingtip appendages connected with this role and is seen just after getting airborne from RAF Lyneham, Wiltshire, on 17 June 1992, during a UK detachment involving international radar trials. This aircraft never saw airline service, being operated as a corporate aircraft all its life. It was originally built in 1957, as a piston-engined Convair 440 for the Bethlehem Steel Corporation, USA, and had its engines changed to become a Convair 580 in September 1965. After a number of company owners, it was delivered to its present operators in July 1973 and is still current.

(*Adrian Balch*)

Opposite above: A typical Gatwick Airport scene in May 1967 – British United Airways' Handley Page Herald Series 201 G-APWF (c/n 154) proudly wears its new BUA blue and tan livery while awaiting its next load of passengers, no doubt bound for Jersey. This aircraft adopted the British Island Airways livery in July 1970, then that of Air UK in January 1980. It was withdrawn from use at Jersey in 1981 and broken up in April 1984.
(*Bob Griggs*)

Opposite below: British Overseas Airways Corporation (BOAC) operated twenty-two Canadair Argonauts, including G-ALHG (c/n 153), which was named *Aurora*. Delivered on 5 July 1949, it gave good service for ten years until being sold to Overseas Aviation in April 1960, who passed it on to Derby Airways the following year. This subsequently became British Midland Airways on 1 October 1964. This aircraft crashed on approach to Ringway Airport, Manchester, on 4 June 1967.
(*Brian Stainer/APN*)

Below: A classic London Heathrow Airport scene was caught on camera in March 1969. G-AVYD, one of BKS Air Transport's three de Havilland Trident 1Es is being turned round by period BEA and BKS vehicles. At this time, BKS Air Transport was a member of the British Air Services group. This aircraft was initially ordered by Channel Airways, but was not delivered and was diverted to BKS on 5 March 1969. The airline changed its name to Northeast Airlines on 1 November 1970, then was absorbed into British Airways on 1 April 1974. However, the following year it was written-off when it skidded off the runway at Bilbao, Spain, on 15 September 1975.
(*Brian Stainer/APN*)

Previous spread: Before Air Niugini was formed in Papua New Guinea, Ansett Airlines of Australia formed a Papua New Guinea subsidiary in October 1936 to link the two countries. By the early 1970s, the fleet included ten Douglas DC-3s, including VH-MAB (c/n 9749) shown here in 1971. This aircraft joined this subsidiary airline on 9 May 1968 and was transferred to the newly-formed Air Niugini on 1 November 1973, becoming P2-MAB. On 13 March 1980, it was sold in the USA and continued in service with a number of private owners.

(Author's collection)

Below: Jersey airline, Intra Airways was formed on 1 January 1969 and operated a total of six Douglas C-47 Dakotas including G-AMPZ (c/n 32872), which is depicted arriving at Staverton Airport, Gloucester, on 20 May 1973. In January 1979, the airline merged with Air Bridge Carriers and G-AMPZ went on to join Clyden Airways, then Harvestair as a pollution sprayer. Today, it still flies in pristine condition with Air Atlantique, in 1998 reverting to its original RAF Transport Command colours as KN442 to celebrate the 50th Anniversary of the Berlin Airlift.

(Adrian Balch)

Opposite above: One of Northeast Airlines' four Trident 1Es, G-AVYC (c/n 2137), is depicted on finals to London Heathrow Airport on a cold, bright winter day on 24 January 1971. Formerly called BKS Air Transport, the airline changed its name to Northeast Airlines on 1 November 1970 and subsequently merged with British Airways on 1 April 1976. This aircraft was withdrawn from use at Heathrow in July 1980 and broken up in May 1981.

(Adrian Balch)

Opposite below: One of the first civilian operators of the Lockheed Hercules was Alaska Airlines. The airline operated two L382E models, including N9227R (c/n 4208), which were known as 'Golden Nugget Freighters' and chartered by mining companies in Alaska. Delivered on 22 March 1967, it continued in service when the airline changed its name to Alaska International Air in November 1972. When it was sold to Saturn Airways in January 1973, it was stretched into a L100-30 model. It was still in service with Southern Air Transport during the 1980s. It is depicted here whilst serving Alaska Airlines at JFK Airport, New York, in May 1970.

(Harry Sievers)

Left: HB-IEL (c/n 5222) was one of four Airspeed As57 Ambassadors operated by the Swiss charter airline, Globe Air. Named *Lalle Keenig*, the aircraft was originally delivered to BEA as G-ALZZ in August 1952. Globe Air bought it in May 1961 and sold it to Autair International in September 1963. It was withdrawn from use at Luton and broken up in May 1969.
(*TAHS*)

Left: Channel Airways operated two Bristol 170 Freighter Mk 21s between September 1957 and August 1966, including G-AICT (c/n 12763). They were purchased for planned vehicle ferry flights from Southend to the continent, but ended up being used for passenger and freight charters.
(*TAHS*)

Above: The Australian internal airline, Ansett-ANA, operated a number of Boeing 727s in competition with those of TAA. VH-RME (c/n 18743) was the airline's second Boeing 727-77 and is seen here in its original Ansett-ANA livery in September 1964, prior to delivery. It was sold to Mexicana in 1979 and, following a number of operators, was finally withdrawn from use at Opa Locka, Florida, in 1994.

(*Boeing*)

Right: Bristol 170 Freighter Mk 21 G-AIFM (c/n 12773), named *City of Carlisle*, was bought by Silver City Airways in October 1951. It went on to serve with British United Air Ferries from 1963 and was broken up at Southend in October 1964. It is seen here being refuelled at Lydd, Kent, in 1961. *(TAHS)*

Right: BAC One-Eleven 416EK G-AVOE (c/n 129) was delivered to Autair International Airways in March 1968, before being sold to Cambrian Airways in December 1969. On 1 April 1976 Cambrian merged with British Airways. *(TAHS)*

Left: Bristol 170 Freighter Mk 31E EC-AHJ (c/n 13129) was delivered new to Iberia as EC-WHJ on 27 June 1953. It was re-registered as seen here, serving on passenger and freight duties until it was sold to Aviaco in 1960. It was withdrawn from use at Valencia after a main-wheel failure on 19 April 1962, which resulted in damage uneconomical to repair.
(*TAHS*)

Above: Airliners at an air show are a rare sight, but the 1998 Biggin Hill International Air Fair featured no less than six piston-engined airliners in the flying display, to celebrate the 50th Anniversary of the Berlin Airlift. The display included G-APSA, one of Atlantic Cargo Airlines' two Douglas DC-6As. Although the DC-6 wasn't used in the Berlin Airlift of 1948, it was wonderfully nostalgic to see it roaring down the crowd line, together with a Lockheed Constellation, two Douglas DC-4s and a DC-3, recalling the Biggin Hill Air Fairs of the early 1960s. Based at Coventry, G-APSA (c/n 45497) was bought from Yemen Airways in February 1987 and is used on cargo charter work, mainly by European car companies for transporting car parts around Europe. It started life in June 1958, when it was delivered to Maritime Central Airways as CF-MCK. It then became G-APSA three months later with Eagle Aviation, which subsequently changed its name to Eagle Airways, Cunard Eagle Airways and then British Eagle International Airlines. It was sold to Saudi Arabian Airlines as HZ-ADA in February 1964, then donated to Yemen Airways in 1971 as 4W-ABQ. Air Atlantique have now operated it for more than ten years. G-APSA was photographed on 7 June 1998, celebrating its fortieth birthday at Biggin Hill, looking as pristine as the day it rolled off the Douglas production line. (See photo on page 20)
(*Adrian Balch*)

Below: Initially, Air Ceylon ordered just one Avro 748, 4R-ACJ (c/n 1571), which was delivered on 27 October 1964. It is seen here during a pre-delivery demonstration at a rather wet Rome, Italy, on 28 October 1964. It didn't survive to see the airline's name change to AirLanka, as it was destroyed by sabotage at Ratmalana Airport on 7 September 1978.
(*Author's collection*)

Opposite above: On 12 April 1963 I-TIVA (c/n 164) was the first of five Handley Page Heralds delivered to Italian charter operator, Aerolinee Itavia. Originally registered G-ASBG, this aircraft served the airline well for more than ten years, before being sold to British Island Airlines in July 1973. Aerolinee Itavia was formed in April 1958 and effectively ceased operations in February 1975. After BIA merged with Air UK on 16 January 1980, this aircraft continued in service until being withdrawn from use at Norwich in September 1981. It was broken up in August 1984.
(*Author's collection*)

Opposite below: Basking in golden autumn sunlight at Southampton-Eastleigh on 12 November 1965 is British United (Channel Islands) Airways' Handley Page Herald Series 201 G-APWI (c/n 157). It was delivered to the airline on 24 May 1963 and served for just over five years, being sold to the Taiwanese operator, Far East Air Transport, as B-2009 in December 1968. Unfortunately, it crashed on 24 February 1969.
(*Clive Moggridge*)

Below: G-ARMX (c/n 1538) was the fifth Avro 748 built and was delivered to Skyways of London in April 1963. On 12 April 1972 Skyways merged with Dan-Air, resulting in this hybrid livery, seen at Bournemouth-Hurn on 29 August 1972. In October 1990, this aircraft was withdrawn from service with Dan-Air and donated to the Manchester Airport Fire Service for training. (*Stephen Wolf*)

Opposite above: Armstrong-Whitworth AW-650 Argosy G-APRL (c/n 6652) was the second of its type to be built and was delivered to Riddle Airlines as N6507R in August 1961. It served in the USA until returning to the UK in July 1973, when it joined Air Bridge Carriers. It is seen here at East Midlands in December 1975 during a brief period when it was leased to Air Anglia. After service with its last operator, Elan Air, it was retired in February 1987 and joined the Midland Air Museum at Coventry. (*Steve Gensler*)

Opposite below: The first colour scheme adopted by the Aviation Traders' Carvair was British United's Channel Air Bridge livery. It is seen on G-ARSD (c/n 2/10311) at Southend shortly after delivery in March 1962. After serving with British Air Ferries, this aircraft was withdrawn from use at Lydd, Kent, in October 1967 and finally broken up in August 1970. Converting a Douglas DC-4 to carry cars was very successful, but only twenty-one conversions were carried out, with only one or two still airworthy in 1998. (*Author's collection*)

Opposite above: Spain's national airline, Iberia, had a large fleet of Caravelles, which numbered seventeen in the early 1970s. There were subtle changes to the livery from the arrival of the first one in February 1962. Caravelle VIR EC-AYE (c/n 198) named *Jose Maria Usandizaga*, was delivered to Iberia on 2 April 1965 and is depicted in the final Iberia colour scheme for the type at Paris-Le Bourget in March 1971. It served all its life with Iberia, being withdrawn from use at Madrid, Spain, in December 1973 and broken up the following year.

(*Author's collection*)

Opposite below: Another airline that operated just three Caravelles was TAP (Transportes Aereos Portugueses), who took delivery of them in 1962. CS-TCC (c/n 137) was the last of TAP's Caravelle VIR trio, which was delivered on 27 November 1962, named *Diu*. It was sold to SAN-Ecuador in November 1975, but was then damaged beyond repair on 12 September 1979. It is seen here taxying out at Zürich, Switzerland, in 1970.

(*Author's collection*)

Below: Seen arriving at Zürich on 19 August 1971 is TS-ITU (c/n 246), one of four Caravelle IIIs operated by Tunis Air. This example was delivered to the airline on 16 February 1968 and was withdrawn from use at Tunis in June 1977.

(*Author's collection*)

Right: This photograph depicts Lockheed L1049G Super Constellation, VT-DJX, of Air India, carrying the legend 'The Flying Sherpa'. Named *Rani of Saguri*, this was one of nine of the type operated by Air India and was delivered in August 1958. A regular visitor to Heathrow over the next two years, it was converted to a freighter in August 1960 and was sold to the Indian Air Force in January 1962 as BG579. It made regular visits to RAF Northolt for another decade before being withdrawn from use and stored at Puna on 31 March 1984.
(*TAHS*)

Right: This is Air Jordan's Douglas DC-6 JY-ACF (c/n 45856), photographed at an unknown location in 1961. It was delivered to American Airlines in November 1946 and in October 1960 was sold to Field Aircraft Service, becoming G-ARFU. Air Jordan bought it in December 1960 but only had it for just under a year. Returning to the US register as N90703, it had several operators before being withdrawn from use at Hal Far, Malta, in August 1980 and broken up.
(*TAHS*)

Top: The background and basic colour scheme gives a clue to the owner of Vickers V.745D Viscount JY-ACI (c/n 240), which wears Jordan Airways titles at Beirut in 1963. It was previously OD-ACU of Middle East Airlines and was leased to Air Jordan from 30 September 1961 until January 1964. It was sold to Air Rhodesia in September 1968 and ended its days being broken up at Harare with Air Zimbabwe in March 1985.
(TAHS)

Above: Douglas C-47B G-AMSV (c/n 16072/32820) still flies today, as part of Air Atlantique's Pollution Control fleet at Coventry. It is seen here at Gatwick in 1968, when in service with Morton Air Services. It retained its basic British United Airways black cheatline from whom it was transferred in November 1962. It was later passed on to several small British airlines and one in France before joining Air Atlantique on 25 March 1982.
(TAHS)

Below: National Airlines' Lockheed Electra N5007K (c/n 1089) taxies in at Los Angeles on 13 November 1966, respendent in its original livery. National was the first airline to order the Electra on 9 December 1955. The initial order for twelve was increased to seventeen and all were disposed of in April 1968. N5007K was delivered on 4 September 1959 and ended is days with the cargo airline, Zantop International, when it crashed at Deadhorse, Alaska, on 30 April 1975.
(*Bernard B. Deatrick*)

Opposite above: The Electra was also very popular 'down under', with both Trans-Australia Airlines and Ansett-ANA operating four each. VH-RMA (c/n 1039) was the first of these and was delivered in February 1959. All were converted as freighters in July 1972 and continued to give excellent service until finally being sold in October 1984. This aircraft was still flying in 1993 as N3560, with leasing company JBQ Aviation Corporation in the USA.
(*Author's collection*)

Opposite below: TEAL (Tasman Empire Airways Limited) took delivery of ZK-TEA (c/n 2005), the first of the four Lockheed Electras, on 15 October 1959. Named *Aotearoa*, it continued in service when the airline changed its name to Air New Zealand on 1 April 1965. The fleet was sold in May 1972. After cargo conversion, this Electra was still flying in 1997 with Fred Olsen Air Transport as LN-FOI. It is seen here when serving with Air New Zealand at Auckland in June 1966.
(*Author's collection*)

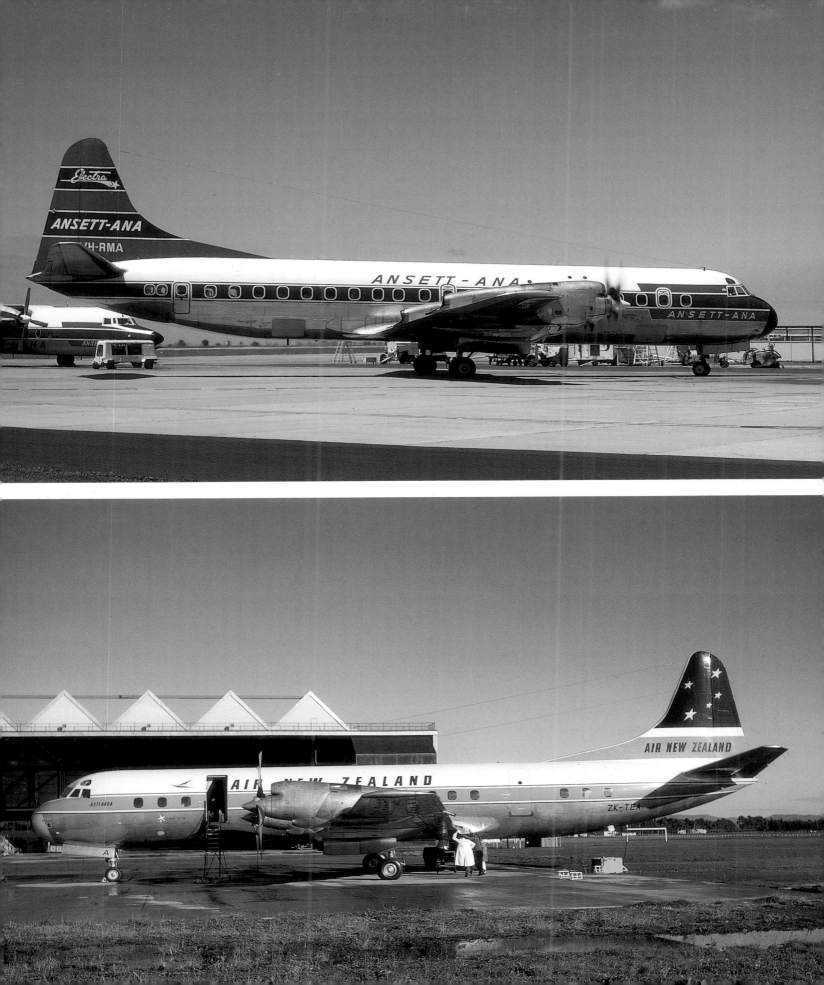

Right: Douglas C-54A Skymaster VR-SEA (c/n 7458) previously served with the USAAF, American Airlines and QANTAS before joining Malayan Airways on lease between September 1958 and April 1960. It is still currently flying in Canada with Buffalo Airways as C-GPSH.
(*TAHS*)

Right: Handley Page HP81 Hermes IV G-ALDU (c/n 20) was delivered to BOAC in October 1950 and was sold to Britavia in May 1954. Following a six-month lease to Kuwait Airways in 1956, it was transferred to Silver City Airways in July 1959, following which the name Britavia disappeared when the airline ceased trading.
(*TAHS*)

Above: A big coup was achieved when Hawker Siddeley sold its Tridents to China. CAAC (Civil Aviation Administration of China) became the Trident's largest export customer, second only to BEA, with orders placed for some thirty-five aircraft. G-BAJM/B-270 was the second of two Super 3Bs orderd by CAAC in November 1972. This was the last Trident to be built and is seen here on a test flight near Hatfield in September 1975, prior to delivery the following month. It is thought to be still in service with the Chinese Air Force, registered 50058.

(*British Aerospace*)

Above: Sudan Airways operated just two Comet 4Cs. These included ST-AAW (c/n 6457), which first flew on 5 November 1962, and is seen here around that time prior to delivery six days later. It was withdrawn from use in October 1973, having served all its life with the airline. It was sold to Dan-Air in June 1975, reverting to its pre-delivery serial G-ASDZ, but never entered service. It was broken up at Lasham in October 1975.

(*British Aerospace*)

Above: The author in the Captain's seat of Sunbird's DC-3, 5Y-AAE, on arrival at the Masai Mara Game Park on 31 March 1986.
(Adrian Balch)

Left: A typical DC-3 cabin scene, as Sunbird Aviation's air hostess, Anna Nzomo attends to passengers in 5Y-AAE en route to Nairobi on 31 March 1986.
(Adrian Balch)

Top : One of Sunbird Aviation's two Douglas DC-3s, 5Y-AAE, awaits passengers at Nairobi's Wilson Airport in March 1986. Sunbird Aviation, which was later merged into Air Kenya, ran a scheduled service with two former East African Airways DC-3s to the Game Parks throughout Kenya for tourists.
(Adrian Balch)

Above: The civil variant of the wartime Lockheed Hudson was the Lodestar, and ZS-ATL was one of two pristine examples operated in South Africa by Commercial Airways (COMAIR). Formed in 1946, COMAIR still operates today as a franchise of British Airways.

(*Author's collection*)

Opposite above: This Fairchild-built F27A Friendship, N2771R (c/n 43) was one of a dozen operated by Pacific Air Lines and was delivered on 2 April 1959, serving the airline until it merged with Air West on 7 March 1968, subsequently becoming Hughes Air West on 1 April 1970. After several operators this aircraft was finally withdrawn from use at Dinard, France, in 1990. It is seen here at San Francisco in February 1968.

(*Terry Waddington*)

Opposite below: This Aeroflot Ilyushin Il-62, SSSR-86653, is in its original livery, though on lease to KLM. It was photographed at Tokyo-Haneda on 25 August 1971, flanked by two Japanese NAMC Y-C11s.

(*Bernard B. Deatrick*)

Above: A dramatic night-time scene was photographed at Southend as British Air Ferries (BAF) Vickers V.806 Viscount G-AOYR (c/n 266) prepared for freight charter. BAF, which became British World Airlines on 6 April 1993, was the last UK operator of the Viscount, retiring its last example in 1997. G-AOYR was delivered new to British European Airways on 11 April 1958, then sold to BKS Air Transport in December 1969, which became Northeast Airlines on 1 November 1970. This airline then merged with British Airways on 1 April 1974. 'Yankee Romeo' was sold to BAF in January 1984 and was leased to British Caledonian Airways for a year, before being returned to BAF in May 1986. The photograph was taken in 1993, two years before the aircraft was withdrawn from use.

(*Courtesy British World Airlines*)

Right: The cockpit of the Vickers Viscount is very different from today's technology. British World Airlines' Captain Colin Towle is seen at the controls of G-APEY en route from Heathrow–Stansted on 18 April 1996, during the last Viscount flight from Heathrow.

(*Adrian Balch*)